THE GREATEST EVER FOR YOUR BUSINESS

TABLE RESERVATIONS BOOK

Activinotes

Activinotes

DAILY JOURNALS, PLANNERS, NOTEBOOKS AND OTHER BLANK BOOKS

Copyright 2016

THIS BOOK

BELONGS TO

_____

Table Reservation Checklist

Date:			Time:			
Table#	Name	# of Persons	Phone #	Arrival	Departure	Status
	1.					
	2.					
	3.					
	4.					
	5.					
	6.					
	7.					
	8.					
	9.					
	10.					
	11.					
	12.					
	13.					
	14.					
	15.					
	16.					
	17.					
	18.					
	19.					
	20.					
	21.					
	22.					
	23.					
	24.					
	25.					
	26.					
	27.					
	28.					

Table Reservation Checklist

Date:			Time:			
Table#	Name	# of Persons	Phone #	Arrival	Departure	Status
	1.					
	2.					
	3.					
	4.					
	5.					
	6.					
	7.					
	8.					
	9.					
	10.					
	11.					
	12.					
	13.					
	14.					
	15.					
	16.					
	17.					
	18.					
	19.					
	20.					
	21.					
	22.					
	23.					
	24.					
	25.					
	26.					
	27.					
	28.					

Table Reservation Checklist

Date:			**Time:**			
Table#	Name	# of Persons	Phone #	Arrival	Departure	Status
	1.					
	2.					
	3.					
	4.					
	5.					
	6.					
	7.					
	8.					
	9.					
	10.					
	11.					
	12.					
	13.					
	14.					
	15.					
	16.					
	17.					
	18.					
	19.					
	20.					
	21.					
	22.					
	23.					
	24.					
	25.					
	26.					
	27.					
	28.					

Table Reservation Checklist

Date:			Time:			
Table#	Name	# of Persons	Phone #	Arrival	Departure	Status
	1.					
	2.					
	3.					
	4.					
	5.					
	6.					
	7.					
	8.					
	9.					
	10.					
	11.					
	12.					
	13.					
	14.					
	15.					
	16.					
	17.					
	18.					
	19.					
	20.					
	21.					
	22.					
	23.					
	24.					
	25.					
	26.					
	27.					
	28.					

Table Reservation Checklist

Date:				Time:			
Table#	Name	# of Persons	Phone #	Arrival	Departure	Status
	1.					
	2.					
	3.					
	4.					
	5.					
	6.					
	7.					
	8.					
	9.					
	10.					
	11.					
	12.					
	13.					
	14.					
	15.					
	16.					
	17.					
	18.					
	19.					
	20.					
	21.					
	22.					
	23.					
	24.					
	25.					
	26.					
	27.					
	28.					

Table Reservation Checklist

Date:				Time:			
Table#	Name	# of Persons	Phone #	Arrival	Departure	Status
	1.					
	2.					
	3.					
	4.					
	5.					
	6.					
	7.					
	8.					
	9.					
	10.					
	11.					
	12.					
	13.					
	14.					
	15.					
	16.					
	17.					
	18.					
	19.					
	20.					
	21.					
	22.					
	23.					
	24.					
	25.					
	26.					
	27.					
	28.					

Table Reservation Checklist

Date:				Time:			
Table#	Name	# of Persons	Phone #	Arrival	Departure	Status
	1.					
	2.					
	3.					
	4.					
	5.					
	6.					
	7.					
	8.					
	9.					
	10.					
	11.					
	12.					
	13.					
	14.					
	15.					
	16.					
	17.					
	18.					
	19.					
	20.					
	21.					
	22.					
	23.					
	24.					
	25.					
	26.					
	27.					
	28.					

Table Reservation Checklist

Date:			Time:			
Table#	Name	# of Persons	Phone #	Arrival	Departure	Status
	1.					
	2.					
	3.					
	4.					
	5.					
	6.					
	7.					
	8.					
	9.					
	10.					
	11.					
	12.					
	13.					
	14.					
	15.					
	16.					
	17.					
	18.					
	19.					
	20.					
	21.					
	22.					
	23.					
	24.					
	25.					
	26.					
	27.					
	28.					

Table Reservation Checklist

Date:			Time:			
Table#	Name	# of Persons	Phone #	Arrival	Departure	Status
	1.					
	2.					
	3.					
	4.					
	5.					
	6.					
	7.					
	8.					
	9.					
	10.					
	11.					
	12.					
	13.					
	14.					
	15.					
	16.					
	17.					
	18.					
	19.					
	20.					
	21.					
	22.					
	23.					
	24.					
	25.					
	26.					
	27.					
	28.					

Table Reservation Checklist

Date:				Time:			

Table#	Name	# of Persons	Phone #	Arrival	Departure	Status
	1.					
	2.					
	3.					
	4.					
	5.					
	6.					
	7.					
	8.					
	9.					
	10.					
	11.					
	12.					
	13.					
	14.					
	15.					
	16.					
	17.					
	18.					
	19.					
	20.					
	21.					
	22.					
	23.					
	24.					
	25.					
	26.					
	27.					
	28.					

Table Reservation Checklist

Date:			Time:			
Table#	Name	# of Persons	Phone #	Arrival	Departure	Status
	1.					
	2.					
	3.					
	4.					
	5.					
	6.					
	7.					
	8.					
	9.					
	10.					
	11.					
	12.					
	13.					
	14.					
	15.					
	16.					
	17.					
	18.					
	19.					
	20.					
	21.					
	22.					
	23.					
	24.					
	25.					
	26.					
	27.					
	28.					

Table Reservation Checklist

Date:			Time:			
Table#	Name	# of Persons	Phone #	Arrival	Departure	Status
	1.					
	2.					
	3.					
	4.					
	5.					
	6.					
	7.					
	8.					
	9.					
	10.					
	11.					
	12.					
	13.					
	14.					
	15.					
	16.					
	17.					
	18.					
	19.					
	20.					
	21.					
	22.					
	23.					
	24.					
	25.					
	26.					
	27.					
	28.					

Table Reservation Checklist

Date:			Time:			
Table#	Name	# of Persons	Phone #	Arrival	Departure	Status
	1.					
	2.					
	3.					
	4.					
	5.					
	6.					
	7.					
	8.					
	9.					
	10.					
	11.					
	12.					
	13.					
	14.					
	15.					
	16.					
	17.					
	18.					
	19.					
	20.					
	21.					
	22.					
	23.					
	24.					
	25.					
	26.					
	27.					
	28.					

Table Reservation Checklist

Date:				Time:		
Table#	Name	# of Persons	Phone #	Arrival	Departure	Status
	1.					
	2.					
	3.					
	4.					
	5.					
	6.					
	7.					
	8.					
	9.					
	10.					
	11.					
	12.					
	13.					
	14.					
	15.					
	16.					
	17.					
	18.					
	19.					
	20.					
	21.					
	22.					
	23.					
	24.					
	25.					
	26.					
	27.					
	28.					

Table Reservation Checklist

Date:			Time:			
Table#	Name	# of Persons	Phone #	Arrival	Departure	Status
	1.					
	2.					
	3.					
	4.					
	5.					
	6.					
	7.					
	8.					
	9.					
	10.					
	11.					
	12.					
	13.					
	14.					
	15.					
	16.					
	17.					
	18.					
	19.					
	20.					
	21.					
	22.					
	23.					
	24.					
	25.					
	26.					
	27.					
	28.					

Table Reservation Checklist

Date:			Time:			
Table#	Name	# of Persons	Phone #	Arrival	Departure	Status
	1.					
	2.					
	3.					
	4.					
	5.					
	6.					
	7.					
	8.					
	9.					
	10.					
	11.					
	12.					
	13.					
	14.					
	15.					
	16.					
	17.					
	18.					
	19.					
	20.					
	21.					
	22.					
	23.					
	24.					
	25.					
	26.					
	27.					
	28.					

Table Reservation Checklist

Date:			Time:			
Table#	Name	# of Persons	Phone #	Arrival	Departure	Status
	1.					
	2.					
	3.					
	4.					
	5.					
	6.					
	7.					
	8.					
	9.					
	10.					
	11.					
	12.					
	13.					
	14.					
	15.					
	16.					
	17.					
	18.					
	19.					
	20.					
	21.					
	22.					
	23.					
	24.					
	25.					
	26.					
	27.					
	28.					

Table Reservation Checklist

Date:			Time:			
Table#	Name	# of Persons	Phone #	Arrival	Departure	Status
	1.					
	2.					
	3.					
	4.					
	5.					
	6.					
	7.					
	8.					
	9.					
	10.					
	11.					
	12.					
	13.					
	14.					
	15.					
	16.					
	17.					
	18.					
	19.					
	20.					
	21.					
	22.					
	23.					
	24.					
	25.					
	26.					
	27.					
	28.					

Table Reservation Checklist

Date:			Time:			
Table#	Name	# of Persons	Phone #	Arrival	Departure	Status
	1.					
	2.					
	3.					
	4.					
	5.					
	6.					
	7.					
	8.					
	9.					
	10.					
	11.					
	12.					
	13.					
	14.					
	15.					
	16.					
	17.					
	18.					
	19.					
	20.					
	21.					
	22.					
	23.					
	24.					
	25.					
	26.					
	27.					
	28.					

Table Reservation Checklist

Date: | Time:

Table#	Name	# of Persons	Phone #	Arrival	Departure	Status
	1.					
	2.					
	3.					
	4.					
	5.					
	6.					
	7.					
	8.					
	9.					
	10.					
	11.					
	12.					
	13.					
	14.					
	15.					
	16.					
	17.					
	18.					
	19.					
	20.					
	21.					
	22.					
	23.					
	24.					
	25.					
	26.					
	27.					
	28.					

Table Reservation Checklist

Date:				Time:			
Table#	Name	# of Persons	Phone #	Arrival	Departure	Status
	1.					
	2.					
	3.					
	4.					
	5.					
	6.					
	7.					
	8.					
	9.					
	10.					
	11.					
	12.					
	13.					
	14.					
	15.					
	16.					
	17.					
	18.					
	19.					
	20.					
	21.					
	22.					
	23.					
	24.					
	25.					
	26.					
	27.					
	28.					

Table Reservation Checklist

Date: _____   Time: _____

Table#	Name	# of Persons	Phone #	Arrival	Departure	Status
	1.					
	2.					
	3.					
	4.					
	5.					
	6.					
	7.					
	8.					
	9.					
	10.					
	11.					
	12.					
	13.					
	14.					
	15.					
	16.					
	17.					
	18.					
	19.					
	20.					
	21.					
	22.					
	23.					
	24.					
	25.					
	26.					
	27.					
	28.					

Table Reservation Checklist

Date:			Time:			
Table#	Name	# of Persons	Phone #	Arrival	Departure	Status
	1.					
	2.					
	3.					
	4.					
	5.					
	6.					
	7.					
	8.					
	9.					
	10.					
	11.					
	12.					
	13.					
	14.					
	15.					
	16.					
	17.					
	18.					
	19.					
	20.					
	21.					
	22.					
	23.					
	24.					
	25.					
	26.					
	27.					
	28.					

Table Reservation Checklist

Date:				Time:		
Table#	Name	# of Persons	Phone #	Arrival	Departure	Status
	1.					
	2.					
	3.					
	4.					
	5.					
	6.					
	7.					
	8.					
	9.					
	10.					
	11.					
	12.					
	13.					
	14.					
	15.					
	16.					
	17.					
	18.					
	19.					
	20.					
	21.					
	22.					
	23.					
	24.					
	25.					
	26.					
	27.					
	28.					

Table Reservation Checklist

Date:				Time:		
Table#	Name	# of Persons	Phone #	Arrival	Departure	Status
	1.					
	2.					
	3.					
	4.					
	5.					
	6.					
	7.					
	8.					
	9.					
	10.					
	11.					
	12.					
	13.					
	14.					
	15.					
	16.					
	17.					
	18.					
	19.					
	20.					
	21.					
	22.					
	23.					
	24.					
	25.					
	26.					
	27.					
	28.					

Table Reservation Checklist

Date:			Time:			
Table#	Name	# of Persons	Phone #	Arrival	Departure	Status
	1.					
	2.					
	3.					
	4.					
	5.					
	6.					
	7.					
	8.					
	9.					
	10.					
	11.					
	12.					
	13.					
	14.					
	15.					
	16.					
	17.					
	18.					
	19.					
	20.					
	21.					
	22.					
	23.					
	24.					
	25.					
	26.					
	27.					
	28.					

Table Reservation Checklist

Date:			Time:			
Table#	Name	# of Persons	Phone #	Arrival	Departure	Status
	1.					
	2.					
	3.					
	4.					
	5.					
	6.					
	7.					
	8.					
	9.					
	10.					
	11.					
	12.					
	13.					
	14.					
	15.					
	16.					
	17.					
	18.					
	19.					
	20.					
	21.					
	22.					
	23.					
	24.					
	25.					
	26.					
	27.					
	28.					

Table Reservation Checklist

Date:			Time:			
Table#	Name	# of Persons	Phone #	Arrival	Departure	Status
	1.					
	2.					
	3.					
	4.					
	5.					
	6.					
	7.					
	8.					
	9.					
	10.					
	11.					
	12.					
	13.					
	14.					
	15.					
	16.					
	17.					
	18.					
	19.					
	20.					
	21.					
	22.					
	23.					
	24.					
	25.					
	26.					
	27.					
	28.					

Table Reservation Checklist

Date:			Time:			
Table#	Name	# of Persons	Phone #	Arrival	Departure	Status
	1.					
	2.					
	3.					
	4.					
	5.					
	6.					
	7.					
	8.					
	9.					
	10.					
	11.					
	12.					
	13.					
	14.					
	15.					
	16.					
	17.					
	18.					
	19.					
	20.					
	21.					
	22.					
	23.					
	24.					
	25.					
	26.					
	27.					
	28.					

Table Reservation Checklist

Date:			Time:			
Table#	Name	# of Persons	Phone #	Arrival	Departure	Status
	1.					
	2.					
	3.					
	4.					
	5.					
	6.					
	7.					
	8.					
	9.					
	10.					
	11.					
	12.					
	13.					
	14.					
	15.					
	16.					
	17.					
	18.					
	19.					
	20.					
	21.					
	22.					
	23.					
	24.					
	25.					
	26.					
	27.					
	28.					

Table Reservation Checklist

Date:			Time:			
Table#	Name	# of Persons	Phone #	Arrival	Departure	Status
	1.					
	2.					
	3.					
	4.					
	5.					
	6.					
	7.					
	8.					
	9.					
	10.					
	11.					
	12.					
	13.					
	14.					
	15.					
	16.					
	17.					
	18.					
	19.					
	20.					
	21.					
	22.					
	23.					
	24.					
	25.					
	26.					
	27.					
	28.					

Table Reservation Checklist

Date:				Time:			
Table#	Name	# of Persons	Phone #	Arrival	Departure	Status
	1.					
	2.					
	3.					
	4.					
	5.					
	6.					
	7.					
	8.					
	9.					
	10.					
	11.					
	12.					
	13.					
	14.					
	15.					
	16.					
	17.					
	18.					
	19.					
	20.					
	21.					
	22.					
	23.					
	24.					
	25.					
	26.					
	27.					
	28.					

Table Reservation Checklist

Date:			Time:			
Table#	Name	# of Persons	Phone #	Arrival	Departure	Status
	1.					
	2.					
	3.					
	4.					
	5.					
	6.					
	7.					
	8.					
	9.					
	10.					
	11.					
	12.					
	13.					
	14.					
	15.					
	16.					
	17.					
	18.					
	19.					
	20.					
	21.					
	22.					
	23.					
	24.					
	25.					
	26.					
	27.					
	28.					

Table Reservation Checklist

Date:			Time:			
Table#	Name	# of Persons	Phone #	Arrival	Departure	Status
	1.					
	2.					
	3.					
	4.					
	5.					
	6.					
	7.					
	8.					
	9.					
	10.					
	11.					
	12.					
	13.					
	14.					
	15.					
	16.					
	17.					
	18.					
	19.					
	20.					
	21.					
	22.					
	23.					
	24.					
	25.					
	26.					
	27.					
	28.					

Table Reservation Checklist

Date:				Time:			

Table#	Name	# of Persons	Phone #	Arrival	Departure	Status
	1.					
	2.					
	3.					
	4.					
	5.					
	6.					
	7.					
	8.					
	9.					
	10.					
	11.					
	12.					
	13.					
	14.					
	15.					
	16.					
	17.					
	18.					
	19.					
	20.					
	21.					
	22.					
	23.					
	24.					
	25.					
	26.					
	27.					
	28.					

Table Reservation Checklist

Date:			Time:			
Table#	Name	# of Persons	Phone #	Arrival	Departure	Status
	1.					
	2.					
	3.					
	4.					
	5.					
	6.					
	7.					
	8.					
	9.					
	10.					
	11.					
	12.					
	13.					
	14.					
	15.					
	16.					
	17.					
	18.					
	19.					
	20.					
	21.					
	22.					
	23.					
	24.					
	25.					
	26.					
	27.					
	28.					

Table Reservation Checklist

Date:			Time:			
Table#	Name	# of Persons	Phone #	Arrival	Departure	Status
	1.					
	2.					
	3.					
	4.					
	5.					
	6.					
	7.					
	8.					
	9.					
	10.					
	11.					
	12.					
	13.					
	14.					
	15.					
	16.					
	17.					
	18.					
	19.					
	20.					
	21.					
	22.					
	23.					
	24.					
	25.					
	26.					
	27.					
	28.					

Table Reservation Checklist

Date:			Time:			
Table#	Name	# of Persons	Phone #	Arrival	Departure	Status
	1.					
	2.					
	3.					
	4.					
	5.					
	6.					
	7.					
	8.					
	9.					
	10.					
	11.					
	12.					
	13.					
	14.					
	15.					
	16.					
	17.					
	18.					
	19.					
	20.					
	21.					
	22.					
	23.					
	24.					
	25.					
	26.					
	27.					
	28.					

Table Reservation Checklist

Date:			Time:			
Table#	Name	# of Persons	Phone #	Arrival	Departure	Status
	1.					
	2.					
	3.					
	4.					
	5.					
	6.					
	7.					
	8.					
	9.					
	10.					
	11.					
	12.					
	13.					
	14.					
	15.					
	16.					
	17.					
	18.					
	19.					
	20.					
	21.					
	22.					
	23.					
	24.					
	25.					
	26.					
	27.					
	28.					

Table Reservation Checklist

Date:			Time:			
Table#	Name	# of Persons	Phone #	Arrival	Departure	Status
	1.					
	2.					
	3.					
	4.					
	5.					
	6.					
	7.					
	8.					
	9.					
	10.					
	11.					
	12.					
	13.					
	14.					
	15.					
	16.					
	17.					
	18.					
	19.					
	20.					
	21.					
	22.					
	23.					
	24.					
	25.					
	26.					
	27.					
	28.					

Table Reservation Checklist

Date:				Time:			

Table#	Name	# of Persons	Phone #	Arrival	Departure	Status
	1.					
	2.					
	3.					
	4.					
	5.					
	6.					
	7.					
	8.					
	9.					
	10.					
	11.					
	12.					
	13.					
	14.					
	15.					
	16.					
	17.					
	18.					
	19.					
	20.					
	21.					
	22.					
	23.					
	24.					
	25.					
	26.					
	27.					
	28.					

Table Reservation Checklist

Date:			Time:			
Table#	Name	# of Persons	Phone #	Arrival	Departure	Status
	1.					
	2.					
	3.					
	4.					
	5.					
	6.					
	7.					
	8.					
	9.					
	10.					
	11.					
	12.					
	13.					
	14.					
	15.					
	16.					
	17.					
	18.					
	19.					
	20.					
	21.					
	22.					
	23.					
	24.					
	25.					
	26.					
	27.					
	28.					

Table Reservation Checklist

Date:			Time:			
Table#	Name	# of Persons	Phone #	Arrival	Departure	Status
	1.					
	2.					
	3.					
	4.					
	5.					
	6.					
	7.					
	8.					
	9.					
	10.					
	11.					
	12.					
	13.					
	14.					
	15.					
	16.					
	17.					
	18.					
	19.					
	20.					
	21.					
	22.					
	23.					
	24.					
	25.					
	26.					
	27.					
	28.					

Table Reservation Checklist

Date:			Time:			
Table#	Name	# of Persons	Phone #	Arrival	Departure	Status
	1.					
	2.					
	3.					
	4.					
	5.					
	6.					
	7.					
	8.					
	9.					
	10.					
	11.					
	12.					
	13.					
	14.					
	15.					
	16.					
	17.					
	18.					
	19.					
	20.					
	21.					
	22.					
	23.					
	24.					
	25.					
	26.					
	27.					
	28.					

Table Reservation Checklist

Date:			Time:			
Table#	Name	# of Persons	Phone #	Arrival	Departure	Status
	1.					
	2.					
	3.					
	4.					
	5.					
	6.					
	7.					
	8.					
	9.					
	10.					
	11.					
	12.					
	13.					
	14.					
	15.					
	16.					
	17.					
	18.					
	19.					
	20.					
	21.					
	22.					
	23.					
	24.					
	25.					
	26.					
	27.					
	28.					

Table Reservation Checklist

Date:			Time:			
Table#	Name	# of Persons	Phone #	Arrival	Departure	Status
	1.					
	2.					
	3.					
	4.					
	5.					
	6.					
	7.					
	8.					
	9.					
	10.					
	11.					
	12.					
	13.					
	14.					
	15.					
	16.					
	17.					
	18.					
	19.					
	20.					
	21.					
	22.					
	23.					
	24.					
	25.					
	26.					
	27.					
	28.					

Table Reservation Checklist

Date:			Time:			
Table#	Name	# of Persons	Phone #	Arrival	Departure	Status
	1.					
	2.					
	3.					
	4.					
	5.					
	6.					
	7.					
	8.					
	9.					
	10.					
	11.					
	12.					
	13.					
	14.					
	15.					
	16.					
	17.					
	18.					
	19.					
	20.					
	21.					
	22.					
	23.					
	24.					
	25.					
	26.					
	27.					
	28.					

Table Reservation Checklist

Date:				Time:			

Table#	Name	# of Persons	Phone #	Arrival	Departure	Status
	1.					
	2.					
	3.					
	4.					
	5.					
	6.					
	7.					
	8.					
	9.					
	10.					
	11.					
	12.					
	13.					
	14.					
	15.					
	16.					
	17.					
	18.					
	19.					
	20.					
	21.					
	22.					
	23.					
	24.					
	25.					
	26.					
	27.					
	28.					

Table Reservation Checklist

Date:			Time:			
Table#	Name	# of Persons	Phone #	Arrival	Departure	Status
	1.					
	2.					
	3.					
	4.					
	5.					
	6.					
	7.					
	8.					
	9.					
	10.					
	11.					
	12.					
	13.					
	14.					
	15.					
	16.					
	17.					
	18.					
	19.					
	20.					
	21.					
	22.					
	23.					
	24.					
	25.					
	26.					
	27.					
	28.					

Table Reservation Checklist

Date:				Time:		
Table#	Name	# of Persons	Phone #	Arrival	Departure	Status
	1.					
	2.					
	3.					
	4.					
	5.					
	6.					
	7.					
	8.					
	9.					
	10.					
	11.					
	12.					
	13.					
	14.					
	15.					
	16.					
	17.					
	18.					
	19.					
	20.					
	21.					
	22.					
	23.					
	24.					
	25.					
	26.					
	27.					
	28.					

Table Reservation Checklist

Date:			Time:			
Table#	Name	# of Persons	Phone #	Arrival	Departure	Status
	1.					
	2.					
	3.					
	4.					
	5.					
	6.					
	7.					
	8.					
	9.					
	10.					
	11.					
	12.					
	13.					
	14.					
	15.					
	16.					
	17.					
	18.					
	19.					
	20.					
	21.					
	22.					
	23.					
	24.					
	25.					
	26.					
	27.					
	28.					

Table Reservation Checklist

Date:				Time:			

Table#	Name	# of Persons	Phone #	Arrival	Departure	Status
	1.					
	2.					
	3.					
	4.					
	5.					
	6.					
	7.					
	8.					
	9.					
	10.					
	11.					
	12.					
	13.					
	14.					
	15.					
	16.					
	17.					
	18.					
	19.					
	20.					
	21.					
	22.					
	23.					
	24.					
	25.					
	26.					
	27.					
	28.					

Table Reservation Checklist

Date:			Time:			
Table#	Name	# of Persons	Phone #	Arrival	Departure	Status
	1.					
	2.					
	3.					
	4.					
	5.					
	6.					
	7.					
	8.					
	9.					
	10.					
	11.					
	12.					
	13.					
	14.					
	15.					
	16.					
	17.					
	18.					
	19.					
	20.					
	21.					
	22.					
	23.					
	24.					
	25.					
	26.					
	27.					
	28.					

Table Reservation Checklist

Date:			Time:			
Table#	Name	# of Persons	Phone #	Arrival	Departure	Status
	1.					
	2.					
	3.					
	4.					
	5.					
	6.					
	7.					
	8.					
	9.					
	10.					
	11.					
	12.					
	13.					
	14.					
	15.					
	16.					
	17.					
	18.					
	19.					
	20.					
	21.					
	22.					
	23.					
	24.					
	25.					
	26.					
	27.					
	28.					

Table Reservation Checklist

Date:			Time:			
Table#	Name	# of Persons	Phone #	Arrival	Departure	Status
	1.					
	2.					
	3.					
	4.					
	5.					
	6.					
	7.					
	8.					
	9.					
	10.					
	11.					
	12.					
	13.					
	14.					
	15.					
	16.					
	17.					
	18.					
	19.					
	20.					
	21.					
	22.					
	23.					
	24.					
	25.					
	26.					
	27.					
	28.					

Table Reservation Checklist

Date:			Time:			
Table#	Name	# of Persons	Phone #	Arrival	Departure	Status
	1.					
	2.					
	3.					
	4.					
	5.					
	6.					
	7.					
	8.					
	9.					
	10.					
	11.					
	12.					
	13.					
	14.					
	15.					
	16.					
	17.					
	18.					
	19.					
	20.					
	21.					
	22.					
	23.					
	24.					
	25.					
	26.					
	27.					
	28.					

Table Reservation Checklist

Date:			Time:			
Table#	Name	# of Persons	Phone #	Arrival	Departure	Status
	1.					
	2.					
	3.					
	4.					
	5.					
	6.					
	7.					
	8.					
	9.					
	10.					
	11.					
	12.					
	13.					
	14.					
	15.					
	16.					
	17.					
	18.					
	19.					
	20.					
	21.					
	22.					
	23.					
	24.					
	25.					
	26.					
	27.					
	28.					

Table Reservation Checklist

Date:			Time:			
Table#	Name	# of Persons	Phone #	Arrival	Departure	Status
	1.					
	2.					
	3.					
	4.					
	5.					
	6.					
	7.					
	8.					
	9.					
	10.					
	11.					
	12.					
	13.					
	14.					
	15.					
	16.					
	17.					
	18.					
	19.					
	20.					
	21.					
	22.					
	23.					
	24.					
	25.					
	26.					
	27.					
	28.					

Table Reservation Checklist

Date:			Time:			
Table#	Name	# of Persons	Phone #	Arrival	Departure	Status
	1.					
	2.					
	3.					
	4.					
	5.					
	6.					
	7.					
	8.					
	9.					
	10.					
	11.					
	12.					
	13.					
	14.					
	15.					
	16.					
	17.					
	18.					
	19.					
	20.					
	21.					
	22.					
	23.					
	24.					
	25.					
	26.					
	27.					
	28.					

Table Reservation Checklist

Date:			Time:			
Table#	Name	# of Persons	Phone #	Arrival	Departure	Status
	1.					
	2.					
	3.					
	4.					
	5.					
	6.					
	7.					
	8.					
	9.					
	10.					
	11.					
	12.					
	13.					
	14.					
	15.					
	16.					
	17.					
	18.					
	19.					
	20.					
	21.					
	22.					
	23.					
	24.					
	25.					
	26.					
	27.					
	28.					

Table Reservation Checklist

Date:			Time:			
Table#	Name	# of Persons	Phone #	Arrival	Departure	Status
	1.					
	2.					
	3.					
	4.					
	5.					
	6.					
	7.					
	8.					
	9.					
	10.					
	11.					
	12.					
	13.					
	14.					
	15.					
	16.					
	17.					
	18.					
	19.					
	20.					
	21.					
	22.					
	23.					
	24.					
	25.					
	26.					
	27.					
	28.					

Table Reservation Checklist

Date:			Time:			
Table#	Name	# of Persons	Phone #	Arrival	Departure	Status
	1.					
	2.					
	3.					
	4.					
	5.					
	6.					
	7.					
	8.					
	9.					
	10.					
	11.					
	12.					
	13.					
	14.					
	15.					
	16.					
	17.					
	18.					
	19.					
	20.					
	21.					
	22.					
	23.					
	24.					
	25.					
	26.					
	27.					
	28.					

Table Reservation Checklist

Date:			Time:			
Table#	Name	# of Persons	Phone #	Arrival	Departure	Status
	1.					
	2.					
	3.					
	4.					
	5.					
	6.					
	7.					
	8.					
	9.					
	10.					
	11.					
	12.					
	13.					
	14.					
	15.					
	16.					
	17.					
	18.					
	19.					
	20.					
	21.					
	22.					
	23.					
	24.					
	25.					
	26.					
	27.					
	28.					

Table Reservation Checklist

Date:			Time:			
Table#	Name	# of Persons	Phone #	Arrival	Departure	Status
	1.					
	2.					
	3.					
	4.					
	5.					
	6.					
	7.					
	8.					
	9.					
	10.					
	11.					
	12.					
	13.					
	14.					
	15.					
	16.					
	17.					
	18.					
	19.					
	20.					
	21.					
	22.					
	23.					
	24.					
	25.					
	26.					
	27.					
	28.					

Table Reservation Checklist

Date:				Time:			
Table#	Name	# of Persons	Phone #	Arrival	Departure	Status
	1.					
	2.					
	3.					
	4.					
	5.					
	6.					
	7.					
	8.					
	9.					
	10.					
	11.					
	12.					
	13.					
	14.					
	15.					
	16.					
	17.					
	18.					
	19.					
	20.					
	21.					
	22.					
	23.					
	24.					
	25.					
	26.					
	27.					
	28.					

Table Reservation Checklist

Date:			Time:			
Table#	Name	# of Persons	Phone #	Arrival	Departure	Status
	1.					
	2.					
	3.					
	4.					
	5.					
	6.					
	7.					
	8.					
	9.					
	10.					
	11.					
	12.					
	13.					
	14.					
	15.					
	16.					
	17.					
	18.					
	19.					
	20.					
	21.					
	22.					
	23.					
	24.					
	25.					
	26.					
	27.					
	28.					

Table Reservation Checklist

Date:			Time:			
Table#	Name	# of Persons	Phone #	Arrival	Departure	Status
	1.					
	2.					
	3.					
	4.					
	5.					
	6.					
	7.					
	8.					
	9.					
	10.					
	11.					
	12.					
	13.					
	14.					
	15.					
	16.					
	17.					
	18.					
	19.					
	20.					
	21.					
	22.					
	23.					
	24.					
	25.					
	26.					
	27.					
	28.					

Table Reservation Checklist

Date: **Time:**

Table#	Name	# of Persons	Phone #	Arrival	Departure	Status
	1.					
	2.					
	3.					
	4.					
	5.					
	6.					
	7.					
	8.					
	9.					
	10.					
	11.					
	12.					
	13.					
	14.					
	15.					
	16.					
	17.					
	18.					
	19.					
	20.					
	21.					
	22.					
	23.					
	24.					
	25.					
	26.					
	27.					
	28.					

Table Reservation Checklist

Date:				Time:		
Table#	**Name**	**# of Persons**	**Phone #**	**Arrival**	**Departure**	**Status**
	1.					
	2.					
	3.					
	4.					
	5.					
	6.					
	7.					
	8.					
	9.					
	10.					
	11.					
	12.					
	13.					
	14.					
	15.					
	16.					
	17.					
	18.					
	19.					
	20.					
	21.					
	22.					
	23.					
	24.					
	25.					
	26.					
	27.					
	28.					

Table Reservation Checklist

Date:			Time:			
Table#	Name	# of Persons	Phone #	Arrival	Departure	Status
	1.					
	2.					
	3.					
	4.					
	5.					
	6.					
	7.					
	8.					
	9.					
	10.					
	11.					
	12.					
	13.					
	14.					
	15.					
	16.					
	17.					
	18.					
	19.					
	20.					
	21.					
	22.					
	23.					
	24.					
	25.					
	26.					
	27.					
	28.					

Table Reservation Checklist

Date:			Time:			
Table#	Name	# of Persons	Phone #	Arrival	Departure	Status
	1.					
	2.					
	3.					
	4.					
	5.					
	6.					
	7.					
	8.					
	9.					
	10.					
	11.					
	12.					
	13.					
	14.					
	15.					
	16.					
	17.					
	18.					
	19.					
	20.					
	21.					
	22.					
	23.					
	24.					
	25.					
	26.					
	27.					
	28.					

Table Reservation Checklist

Date:			Time:			
Table#	Name	# of Persons	Phone #	Arrival	Departure	Status
	1.					
	2.					
	3.					
	4.					
	5.					
	6.					
	7.					
	8.					
	9.					
	10.					
	11.					
	12.					
	13.					
	14.					
	15.					
	16.					
	17.					
	18.					
	19.					
	20.					
	21.					
	22.					
	23.					
	24.					
	25.					
	26.					
	27.					
	28.					

Table Reservation Checklist

Date:			Time:			
Table#	Name	# of Persons	Phone #	Arrival	Departure	Status
	1.					
	2.					
	3.					
	4.					
	5.					
	6.					
	7.					
	8.					
	9.					
	10.					
	11.					
	12.					
	13.					
	14.					
	15.					
	16.					
	17.					
	18.					
	19.					
	20.					
	21.					
	22.					
	23.					
	24.					
	25.					
	26.					
	27.					
	28.					

Table Reservation Checklist

Date:				Time:		
Table#	Name	# of Persons	Phone #	Arrival	Departure	Status
	1.					
	2.					
	3.					
	4.					
	5.					
	6.					
	7.					
	8.					
	9.					
	10.					
	11.					
	12.					
	13.					
	14.					
	15.					
	16.					
	17.					
	18.					
	19.					
	20.					
	21.					
	22.					
	23.					
	24.					
	25.					
	26.					
	27.					
	28.					

Table Reservation Checklist

Date:			Time:			
Table#	Name	# of Persons	Phone #	Arrival	Departure	Status
	1.					
	2.					
	3.					
	4.					
	5.					
	6.					
	7.					
	8.					
	9.					
	10.					
	11.					
	12.					
	13.					
	14.					
	15.					
	16.					
	17.					
	18.					
	19.					
	20.					
	21.					
	22.					
	23.					
	24.					
	25.					
	26.					
	27.					
	28.					

Table Reservation Checklist

Date:			Time:			
Table#	Name	# of Persons	Phone #	Arrival	Departure	Status
	1.					
	2.					
	3.					
	4.					
	5.					
	6.					
	7.					
	8.					
	9.					
	10.					
	11.					
	12.					
	13.					
	14.					
	15.					
	16.					
	17.					
	18.					
	19.					
	20.					
	21.					
	22.					
	23.					
	24.					
	25.					
	26.					
	27.					
	28.					

Table Reservation Checklist

Date:			Time:			
Table#	Name	# of Persons	Phone #	Arrival	Departure	Status
	1.					
	2.					
	3.					
	4.					
	5.					
	6.					
	7.					
	8.					
	9.					
	10.					
	11.					
	12.					
	13.					
	14.					
	15.					
	16.					
	17.					
	18.					
	19.					
	20.					
	21.					
	22.					
	23.					
	24.					
	25.					
	26.					
	27.					
	28.					

Table Reservation Checklist

Date:			Time:			
Table#	Name	# of Persons	Phone #	Arrival	Departure	Status
	1.					
	2.					
	3.					
	4.					
	5.					
	6.					
	7.					
	8.					
	9.					
	10.					
	11.					
	12.					
	13.					
	14.					
	15.					
	16.					
	17.					
	18.					
	19.					
	20.					
	21.					
	22.					
	23.					
	24.					
	25.					
	26.					
	27.					
	28.					

Table Reservation Checklist

Date:			Time:			
Table#	Name	# of Persons	Phone #	Arrival	Departure	Status
	1.					
	2.					
	3.					
	4.					
	5.					
	6.					
	7.					
	8.					
	9.					
	10.					
	11.					
	12.					
	13.					
	14.					
	15.					
	16.					
	17.					
	18.					
	19.					
	20.					
	21.					
	22.					
	23.					
	24.					
	25.					
	26.					
	27.					
	28.					

Table Reservation Checklist

Date:			Time:			
Table#	Name	# of Persons	Phone #	Arrival	Departure	Status
	1.					
	2.					
	3.					
	4.					
	5.					
	6.					
	7.					
	8.					
	9.					
	10.					
	11.					
	12.					
	13.					
	14.					
	15.					
	16.					
	17.					
	18.					
	19.					
	20.					
	21.					
	22.					
	23.					
	24.					
	25.					
	26.					
	27.					
	28.					

Table Reservation Checklist

Date:			Time:			
Table#	Name	# of Persons	Phone #	Arrival	Departure	Status
	1.					
	2.					
	3.					
	4.					
	5.					
	6.					
	7.					
	8.					
	9.					
	10.					
	11.					
	12.					
	13.					
	14.					
	15.					
	16.					
	17.					
	18.					
	19.					
	20.					
	21.					
	22.					
	23.					
	24.					
	25.					
	26.					
	27.					
	28.					

Table Reservation Checklist

Date:			Time:			
Table#	Name	# of Persons	Phone #	Arrival	Departure	Status
	1.					
	2.					
	3.					
	4.					
	5.					
	6.					
	7.					
	8.					
	9.					
	10.					
	11.					
	12.					
	13.					
	14.					
	15.					
	16.					
	17.					
	18.					
	19.					
	20.					
	21.					
	22.					
	23.					
	24.					
	25.					
	26.					
	27.					
	28.					

Table Reservation Checklist

Date:			Time:			
Table#	Name	# of Persons	Phone #	Arrival	Departure	Status
	1.					
	2.					
	3.					
	4.					
	5.					
	6.					
	7.					
	8.					
	9.					
	10.					
	11.					
	12.					
	13.					
	14.					
	15.					
	16.					
	17.					
	18.					
	19.					
	20.					
	21.					
	22.					
	23.					
	24.					
	25.					
	26.					
	27.					
	28.					

Table Reservation Checklist

Date:			Time:			
Table#	Name	# of Persons	Phone #	Arrival	Departure	Status
	1.					
	2.					
	3.					
	4.					
	5.					
	6.					
	7.					
	8.					
	9.					
	10.					
	11.					
	12.					
	13.					
	14.					
	15.					
	16.					
	17.					
	18.					
	19.					
	20.					
	21.					
	22.					
	23.					
	24.					
	25.					
	26.					
	27.					
	28.					

Table Reservation Checklist

Table#	Name	# of Persons	Phone #	Arrival	Departure	Status
Date:			Time:			
	1.					
	2.					
	3.					
	4.					
	5.					
	6.					
	7.					
	8.					
	9.					
	10.					
	11.					
	12.					
	13.					
	14.					
	15.					
	16.					
	17.					
	18.					
	19.					
	20.					
	21.					
	22.					
	23.					
	24.					
	25.					
	26.					
	27.					
	28.					

Table Reservation Checklist

Date:			Time:			
Table#	Name	# of Persons	Phone #	Arrival	Departure	Status
	1.					
	2.					
	3.					
	4.					
	5.					
	6.					
	7.					
	8.					
	9.					
	10.					
	11.					
	12.					
	13.					
	14.					
	15.					
	16.					
	17.					
	18.					
	19.					
	20.					
	21.					
	22.					
	23.					
	24.					
	25.					
	26.					
	27.					
	28.					

Table Reservation Checklist

Date:				Time:		
Table#	Name	# of Persons	Phone #	Arrival	Departure	Status
	1.					
	2.					
	3.					
	4.					
	5.					
	6.					
	7.					
	8.					
	9.					
	10.					
	11.					
	12.					
	13.					
	14.					
	15.					
	16.					
	17.					
	18.					
	19.					
	20.					
	21.					
	22.					
	23.					
	24.					
	25.					
	26.					
	27.					
	28.					

Table Reservation Checklist

Date:			Time:			
Table#	Name	# of Persons	Phone #	Arrival	Departure	Status
	1.					
	2.					
	3.					
	4.					
	5.					
	6.					
	7.					
	8.					
	9.					
	10.					
	11.					
	12.					
	13.					
	14.					
	15.					
	16.					
	17.					
	18.					
	19.					
	20.					
	21.					
	22.					
	23.					
	24.					
	25.					
	26.					
	27.					
	28.					

Table Reservation Checklist

Date:				Time:			
Table#	Name	# of Persons	Phone #	Arrival	Departure	Status
	1.					
	2.					
	3.					
	4.					
	5.					
	6.					
	7.					
	8.					
	9.					
	10.					
	11.					
	12.					
	13.					
	14.					
	15.					
	16.					
	17.					
	18.					
	19.					
	20.					
	21.					
	22.					
	23.					
	24.					
	25.					
	26.					
	27.					
	28.					

Table Reservation Checklist

Date:			Time:			
Table#	Name	# of Persons	Phone #	Arrival	Departure	Status
	1.					
	2.					
	3.					
	4.					
	5.					
	6.					
	7.					
	8.					
	9.					
	10.					
	11.					
	12.					
	13.					
	14.					
	15.					
	16.					
	17.					
	18.					
	19.					
	20.					
	21.					
	22.					
	23.					
	24.					
	25.					
	26.					
	27.					
	28.					

Table Reservation Checklist

Date:			Time:			
Table#	Name	# of Persons	Phone #	Arrival	Departure	Status
	1.					
	2.					
	3.					
	4.					
	5.					
	6.					
	7.					
	8.					
	9.					
	10.					
	11.					
	12.					
	13.					
	14.					
	15.					
	16.					
	17.					
	18.					
	19.					
	20.					
	21.					
	22.					
	23.					
	24.					
	25.					
	26.					
	27.					
	28.					

Table Reservation Checklist

Date:			Time:			
Table#	Name	# of Persons	Phone #	Arrival	Departure	Status
	1.					
	2.					
	3.					
	4.					
	5.					
	6.					
	7.					
	8.					
	9.					
	10.					
	11.					
	12.					
	13.					
	14.					
	15.					
	16.					
	17.					
	18.					
	19.					
	20.					
	21.					
	22.					
	23.					
	24.					
	25.					
	26.					
	27.					
	28.					

Table Reservation Checklist

Date:			Time:			
Table#	Name	# of Persons	Phone #	Arrival	Departure	Status
	1.					
	2.					
	3.					
	4.					
	5.					
	6.					
	7.					
	8.					
	9.					
	10.					
	11.					
	12.					
	13.					
	14.					
	15.					
	16.					
	17.					
	18.					
	19.					
	20.					
	21.					
	22.					
	23.					
	24.					
	25.					
	26.					
	27.					
	28.					

Table Reservation Checklist

Date:				Time:		
Table#	Name	# of Persons	Phone #	Arrival	Departure	Status
	1.					
	2.					
	3.					
	4.					
	5.					
	6.					
	7.					
	8.					
	9.					
	10.					
	11.					
	12.					
	13.					
	14.					
	15.					
	16.					
	17.					
	18.					
	19.					
	20.					
	21.					
	22.					
	23.					
	24.					
	25.					
	26.					
	27.					
	28.					

Table Reservation Checklist

Date:			Time:			
Table#	Name	# of Persons	Phone #	Arrival	Departure	Status
	1.					
	2.					
	3.					
	4.					
	5.					
	6.					
	7.					
	8.					
	9.					
	10.					
	11.					
	12.					
	13.					
	14.					
	15.					
	16.					
	17.					
	18.					
	19.					
	20.					
	21.					
	22.					
	23.					
	24.					
	25.					
	26.					
	27.					
	28.					

www.ingramcontent.com/pod-product-compliance
Lightning Source LLC
Chambersburg PA
CBHW081337090426
42737CB00017B/3181